Captain James Cook,
Explorer

by Cynthia Clampitt

Editorial Offices: Glenview, Illinois • Parsippany, New Jersey • New York, New York

Sales Offices: Needham, Massachusetts • Duluth, Georgia • Glenview, Illinois
Coppell, Texas • Ontario, California • Mesa, Arizona

The World's Explorer

Unlike most of the great British leaders of the 1700s, James Cook did not come from a wealthy or powerful family. As a result, he had to work harder than many other officers in the British navy. But he was smart and worked hard to develop his abilities. By the time he died, he had completely changed the map of the world. He had traveled farther than anyone else had ever done—but that was just part of what he achieved.

James Cook spent most of his adult life sailing the world's oceans.

James Cook was born in a cottage in northern England on October 27, 1728, similar to this one.

Young James Cook

James Cook was born in a small farming village in northern England. His father was a poor farmworker from Scotland. Fortunately for James, a farmer who hired his father noticed how smart James was, and the farmer offered to send James to school. From the age of eight to the age of twelve, James studied reading, writing, and arithmetic. He still had to help his father on the farm, but he spent his free time studying.

When Cook was sixteen, he got a job at a store in a nearby village. The village was not far from Whitby, a busy port filled with ships. Cook saw the ships every day. He talked to the sailors.

Life at Sea Begins

The teenaged James Cook was a good worker, but the shopkeeper could see that he was more interested in the ships than in the store. After a year and a half, the shopkeeper introduced Cook to a ship owner in Whitby. Cook's life at sea had begun.

Cook spent the next eight years learning about ships and sailing. The Whitby ships sailed the dangerous waters of the North Sea. Learning to sail there equipped Cook to sail anywhere.

Cook's skills and knowledge grew. He also grew in height and was now more than six feet tall. He was offered a promotion in Whitby, but he thought that the British navy would offer him more opportunities to see the world.

It was here, in the English town of Whitby, that Cook first came in contact with ships and the sea.

The Seven Years' War

The Seven Years' War lasted from 1756 to 1763, although the North American part of the war began in 1754. It involved all of the major European powers of that time. Much of the war took place in Europe, but not all. The part of this war fought in North America is known in the United States as the French and Indian War.

Life in the Royal Navy was not easy. Ships were crowded and trips were long. Many sailors died of **scurvy**, a disease caused by a lack of vitamin C. Cook did not like everything he saw, but he obeyed orders and worked hard.

Soon Cook had command of his own ship. The Seven Years' War had begun, and Cook was sent to defend the northern coast of England. Then in 1757 he was ordered to go to Canada. He created charts of the St. Lawrence River that helped England win the war in Canada.

After the war, Cook spent summers mapping eastern Canada. But it was a scientific report he wrote that made people begin to notice him. Most naval officers did not write about the Sun and the planets!

In Tahiti, people paddled their large canoes out to greet Cook's ship. Detailed drawings made during the voyage show us what Cook and his crew saw as they traveled.

Cook's Exploring Begins

Many people in Britain thought that exploring the unknown parts of the world was important. The British navy began to realize that James Cook's abilities made him perfect for this work. He was a skilled sailor, a scientist, a writer, an artist, a mathematician, an explorer, and a mapmaker. Cook was asked to make a long **voyage**, or journey by sea, to the far side of the Earth.

First Cook and his crew would go to Tahiti, for a scientific project. Then they were expected to explore the southern **latitudes** to see if there was another continent south of the **equator**.

In August 1768 James Cook set sail in a ship called the *Endeavour*. Remembering the things that he did not like about his early days in the Royal Navy, Cook insisted on cleanliness on the ship and a healthful diet for his crew.

Cook found and charted New Zealand, a difficult project that took six months to complete. Heading west, he came to and mapped the east coast of Australia. Sailing north, he charted the 2,000-mile-long coast as well. Many discoveries were made. The botanists, or plant scientists, on the voyage discovered so many new plants in one place that Cook named the spot Botany Bay.

In 1771 the *Endeavour* headed back toward England. All of Cook's achievements were important, but one was a real surprise: in three years at sea, Cook had not lost anyone to scurvy. This had never happened before. Cook's ideas about health and diet had been correct.

This stamp from 1940 shows Cook; his ship, the *Endeavour*; and his chart of New Zealand.

Cook's Second Voyage

In the 1700s many people in the **Northern Hemisphere** believed that there must be another continent in the **Southern Hemisphere**. Cook had only been home for one year, but he was asked to go on another voyage.

On this voyage, Cook's ship was the *Resolution*. The *Adventure* was the second ship on this voyage. He sailed south from England into the **frigid** waters around Antarctica. Cook and his crew were the first people to travel south of the Antarctic Circle.

Cook felt certain that there was land under the ice. Though this was not the giant continent people expected him to find, he believed that this was the last continent that would be discovered in the Southern Hemisphere. He was right.

As Cook sailed closer to Antarctica, the terrible cold froze the ships' ropes and sails, making work nearly impossible. Surrounded by broken ice and towering icebergs, the ships were in constant danger of being crushed. They tried several times to reach land, but they only got within one hundred miles of Antarctica's coast. The cold was too great, and they were forced to give up.

Artists on Cook's voyages created pictures of what the explorers saw. Here, Cook's ship is seen among icebergs near Antarctica. Men from the ship have taken small boats out to collect ice to melt for water.

Cook headed into the South Pacific, where he mapped several islands, including Tonga, Rapa Nui (Easter Island), Fiji, and the New Hebrides. But eventually, he turned back toward Antarctica, sailing all the rest of the way around the frozen continent before heading back to England.

Cook reached home in July 1775. This second voyage had taken more than three years and had covered seventy thousand miles.

The Third Voyage

People still wondered whether there was a Northwest Passage, an ocean passage above North America connecting the Atlantic and Pacific Oceans. James Cook was now forty-seven years old and his health was not good. But he understood how important the discovery of this passage would be to Britain. He said yes to another voyage and departed in July 1776.

Cook again sailed on the *Resolution*, but there was also a second ship, the *Discovery*. The two ships sailed south of Africa and into the Pacific Ocean. As they traveled north, they found many new islands, including the Hawaiian Islands. From Hawaii, Cook headed for North America. He explored and mapped the coast of what is now Oregon, Washington, and Alaska.

Cook sailed into the Arctic Ocean. Ahead of him were massive walls of ice. Cook got as close to the ice walls as he could, but there was no passage through to the Atlantic. Disappointed, Cook turned west. He charted part of Siberia, but winter was coming.

Cook felt that warm weather would be healthy for his crew, so he decided to return to Hawaii. He and his crews were welcomed by the Hawaiians at first, though tensions grew because of misunderstandings.

In January Cook again sailed toward the Arctic Ocean to search for a way through. But one of the ships was damaged in a storm and he was forced to return to Hawaii. This time the Hawaiians were not glad to see Cook and his men return. On February 14, 1779, several Hawaiian warriors stabbed Cook to death. His saddened crew sailed back to England with the news.

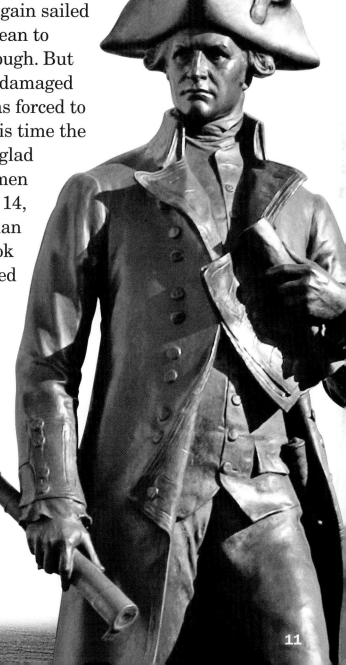

James Cook is still honored today in England. This statue of Cook stands in central London.

Science and Mathematics

James Cook is remembered today not only for his famous voyages but also for his contributions in the fields of science and mathematics. He loved to learn. In addition to learning about ships, he also studied mathematics and science. One of his favorite sciences was astronomy, the study of the Sun, stars, and planets. He also studied health and nutrition, which helped him discover a way to prevent scurvy. Scurvy was the number one cause of death on long voyages in the 1700s. His success in stopping scurvy among his crews was seen as being almost a miracle.

Cook's skill in mathematics helped him in many ways. In Canada during the Seven Years' War, Cook met a man who taught him the science of surveying, which is the careful measuring of the size, shape, and location of places. Surveying was a new science, but Cook realized that it would become an important one. He studied hard and was soon a skilled surveyor. This science, combined with his knowledge of mathematics, made it possible for Cook to create very accurate charts and maps of all the places he visited.

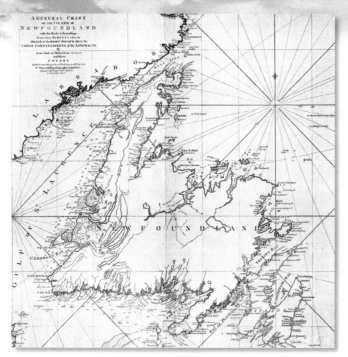

Because Cook had studied mathematics and surveying, he was able to make accurate, detailed maps, such as this one of Newfoundland.

Because of his knowledge of astronomy, Cook was given a scientific assignment for his first voyage. While in Tahiti he was to observe the planet Venus passing in front of the Sun. Timing this event would help scientists calculate the distance between Earth and the Sun.

On his second voyage, Cook was given another assignment that used his mathematical skills. While latitude had been measured, **longitude** had never been accurately measured. When Cook departed in July 1772, he took with him the first clock that would work on a ship. This clock could be used to figure out longitude. It helped Cook to accurately identify the location of many places. This was important on the ocean, where there are no landmarks.

James Cook, Writer

In addition to studying and exploring, James Cook also wrote about everything he learned, saw, or experienced. It was because of a paper he wrote about the Sun and Moon that he first came to the attention of Britain's scientists. This was why he was asked to make the trip to Tahiti. He won an award for the scientific paper he wrote about stopping scurvy.

A picture of Cook from his book, *A Voyage Toward the South Pole*

Sailing Near Antarctica: From Captain Cook's Journal

"The clouds near the horizon were of a perfect snow whiteness and were difficult to distinguish from the ice hills whose lofty [high] summits reached the clouds. The outer or northern edge of this immense ice field was composed of loose or broken ice so close packed together that nothing could enter it... In this field we counted ninety-seven ice hills or mountains."

In addition to his scientific reports, Cook kept journals of all his trips. This is why we know so much about his voyages. He recorded in great detail the plants that were discovered, the animals that were seen, the activities of the people they met, and the land and sea around them.

Cook's writing makes it possible for readers to "travel" along with him on his amazing voyages. Cook's explorations changed the map of the world.

Glossary

equator the imaginary line that circles the center of Earth from east to west

frigid very cold

latitude the measurement of how far north or south of the equator a place is located

longitude the measurement of how far east or west of the prime meridian a place is located

Northern Hemisphere the half of Earth north of the equator

scurvy a disease caused by a lack of vitamin C

Southern Hemisphere the half of Earth south of the equator

voyage a journey by sea